Dinas Brân

THE VALES OF CLWYD AND LLANGOLLEN

A Historical Guide
by
Michael Senior

Note
Some of this material has been published before, in my earlier books
Disputed Border and *The Story of the Dee in Wales.*

First edition: 2013

ISBN: 978-1-84527-455-9

Cover design: Carreg Gwalch

Published by Gwasg Carreg Gwalch,
12 Iard yr Orsaf, Llanrwst, Wales LL26 0EH
tel: 01492 642031
fax: 01492 641502
email: books@carreg-gwalch.com
website: www.carreg-gwalch.com

Contents

Walking on the Clwydian Hills

Introduction

The long line of soft heather-covered summits known as the Clwydian hills forms one of the distinctive approaches to northern Wales. Not surprisingly, several iron age defensive hillforts are sited on its summits. Below lies the beautiful mature landscape of the Vale of Clwyd. At one end of this, the Horseshoe Pass sweeps dramatically over Llantysilio mountain to pitch down into the valley of the Dee, a world itself abundant in cultural and industrial history, puctuated by the travellers' towns of Corwen and Llangollen.

Since November 2011 the whole of this has been recognised as a unit by the extension of the 'Clwydian Range Area of Outstanding Natural Beauty'. This now includes an area covering much of the Dee valley and running as far as the Ceiriog valley, and so encompasses such magnificent features, natural and man-made, as the Eglwyseg escarpment, the Horseshoe Pass, Pontcysyllte aqueduct, Valle Crucis Abbey and Chirk Castle.

The summit of Moel Fama

Moel Arthur

5

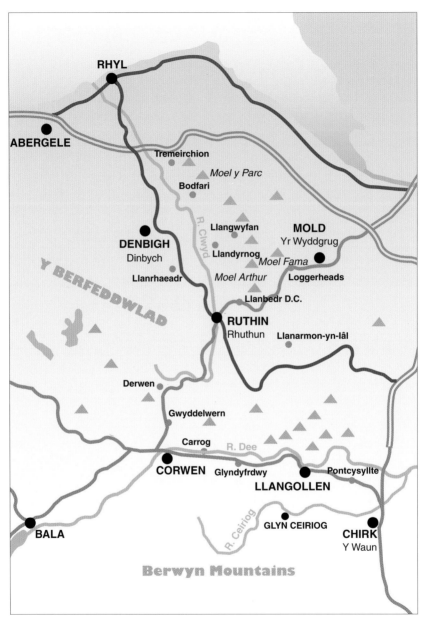

Map of the Clwyd and Ceiriog valleys,
showing the medieval heartland of Berfeddwlad

Chapter 1

THE MIDDLE COUNTRY

Hazel and elder are collapsed into a broad leaf-filled ditch, choked in summer with flies and brambles, thick with fallen leaves in winter: wherever it lurks at the edges of our area, and when it occasionally intrudes into that, this is the form most characteristically taken here by Offa's Dyke. It serves accidentally as an apt image of the confused nature here of this no-man's land, the shared borderland of England and Wales, of those unstated and undefined assumptions which lie behind the character of this piece of Britain.

But this is called the Middle Country, *Y Berfeddwlad*, for a different reason. Perfedd means middle in the sense of being at the heart and core of something, as well as being perhaps at its physical centre, so that we may sense an emotional attachment to this much-disputed area. Yet it bore no special status, either at the time when Wales was made of separate kingdoms, or when it was more or less unified under the independent princes, when Wales was divided into the units of local administration of *cantref* ('hundred') and *cwmwd/cymydau* (translated as 'commote/s') which the Princes had received from the early medieval form derived from the tribal holdings, and which was disturbed only by the conquest of Wales which imposed the Norman form of 'lordships' on it as an overall layer.

The kingdom, or *Gwlad*, was composed of a number of *cantrefi*, which were each composed of *cymydau*. But the Perfeddwlad was never any of these, being not even a kingdom in its own right, and in fact called 'middle' because it lay between two kingdoms, Gwynedd and Powys. Technically within Gwynedd, it was the area bordered by the river Conwy on the east and the river Dee on the south, and hard against the English border on the east, and it consisted of the four catrefs of Rhos,

Rhufuniog, Tegeingl and Dyffryn Clwyd, with the commote of Dinmael, actually part of Powys, traditionally added on.

Here, in this book, we are concerned with only part of this land, the cantrefs of Dyffryn Clwyd and Rhufoniog, and with some of Powys to their south. These, it must be said, do not bear the consistency implied by their historical background, but rather differ through a basic geographical distinction.

Essentially they are two different sorts of river valley. The river Clwyd lies in a vast silt plain, flat-bottomed and wide through being the depository of river mud, the topsoil carried from other slopes and laid out evenly here by endless floods. The Dee runs winding, where it heads towards Llangollen, through a fault in the limestone, giving tall steep-sided hillsides bounding it, and a resulting feeling of containment, of enclosure. It is hardly surprising if the two areas have developed different characters, and with them ways of life. Different again, to both of them, is the third valley which is included here because it forms a trio with its neighbours, and because it would be a shame to leave it out: the wilder, more elusive Ceiriog valley, which would be a side-shoot of the Dee valley if it were not separated from it, to form a world of its own, by the mass of the Berwyn mountains.

The rich soil of the Clwyd valley has given rise, over the centuries, to a settled way of life based on substantial farms and great estates. The defile of the Dee at Llangollen provides a way into Wales, and so a route much used by travellers, and, incidentally, a landscape abundant in the picturesque.

The Ceiriog is not so easily categorised, and fits less easily into a pattern. It is self-defining, and so really has to be seen to be understood.

Although the whole area is within miles of the English border, many aspects of it could hardly be more Welsh. Welshness has countless facets; it is by no means a simple thing; and here we have three quite distinctive aspects of it.

Vale of Clwyd and the distant hills

Moel Arthur – one of the Clwydian Hills bears the King's name is also the site of a Celtic hilltop fort

9

St Beuno's college

*Bryn Bella gateway
at Tremeirchion*

Gerard Manley Hopkins

Chapter 2

BENEATH THE CLWYDIAN HILLS

From the front of the college of St. Beuno you can see the Vale and its context, bounded in the far distance by the Carneddau, by the sea and by the Ormes heads, and in between, nearer at hand, utterly peaceful, a settled land of field-patterned farms, luxuriant with hedgerow trees and randomly dotted scattered settlements. The rare church towers provide location points in this broadness, a generous extent which is in effect the flood-plain of not just the Clwyd, but also of the Elwy, and of the Wheeler converged a little higher up.

> Lovely the woods, waters, meadows, combes, vales,
> All the air things wear that build this world of Wales.

Gerard Manley Hopkins, the most innovative English poet of the nineteenth century, was greatly influenced by his time at St. Beuno's, where, between the years 1874 and 1877, he studied for the priesthood as a Jesuit. He was thus there when in 1875 he heard of the wreck of the Deutschland, which inspired his probably greatest poem:

> Away in the loveable west,
> On a pastoral forehead of Wales,
> I was under a roof here, I was at rest,
> And they the prey of the gales;

Though born in Essex, and educated at Highgate School and Oxford, Hopkins responded sympathetically to the Welsh surroundings in which he lived during this influential period. His innate love of nature thrived on this hillside overlooking the deeply rural vale, and his study of Welsh verse was a factor in his discovery of new rhythms.

St. Beuno's was built in 1848 by the Jesuits, who owned the farmland on which it stands, as a place of study. Jesuits training for the priesthood spent a period there studying theology. It is still in much the same use by the same order, being now a place of retreat – offering periods of prayer and contemplation – known now as an 'Ignatian Spirituality Centre'. Though simple and functional inside, very much like a school, with its plain rooms and corridors, the building outside is of some architectural interest, having been designed by Joseph Hansom, who was also responsible for Birmingham Town Hall. Hansom ironically became best known to posterity through registering a patent on a 'Safety Cab', in 1834. As a result of the distinguished connection to him the outside of St. Beuno's bears some discreet Gothic features, worthy of this period of fine architecture.

St. Beuno's is in the land of country lanes, the winding hedge-enclosed descendants of farm tracks, but the road past it eventually makes contact with a route into the heart of the vale at the next village, **Tremeirchion.**

It is strange, and not otherwise characteristic of this area, that so short a distance down the road we should immediately come across another English literary connection.

Mrs. Thrale is best known to us as the friend of the great Doctor Johnson – and indeed it is unlikely that she would be known to us at all without that link. Indeed this is even commemorated inside Tremeirchion's church of Corpus Christi, where a plaque refers to her as 'Dr. Johnson's Mrs. Thrale', though it fairly adds that she was witty, vivacious and charming, and that 'in an age of Genius She held ever a foremost Place'.

Hester's connection with the area of Denbighshire is explained by the fact that she was a Salusbury, so a member of a family with a long-standing landowning history in this part of Wales. The family home, Lleweni, is now no more than a farmhouse, the massive 'palace' having been demolished in the 19th century to provide material for the building of Kinmel Hall. It lies in the middle of the flood-plain of the Clwyd, not far from Denbigh and just south of Bodfari, an odd place, it seems, to found a stately

Hester Thrale   *Samuel Johnson*

Corpus Cristi church, Tremeirchion

13

Bach y Graig

Lleweni as it is seen today

home, close by the river on a perpetual flood hazard, where the wide, abundant valley still becomes a lake of linking water-meadows several times a year. A holiday complex, with gliding operation, now occupies part of the palace's former grounds. Another property which became Salusbury territory is that of Bach y Graig, which is right here around Tremeirchion.

The precise distant origin of the family is unsure, but there were Salusburys at Lleweni before the 1330s, and by the late 15th century they had emerged, by then widespread landowners, as prominent supporters of the Tudor monarchy. They held in succession every notable office in the north Wales area, and also suffered equivalent setbacks and animosity, but a branch of the family retained into the 18th century the lands at Bach y Graig, which passed to Hester from her father, one of many John Salusburys.

He, however, became bankrupt, through a major speculation in Canada, and we might not have heard any more of her had she not moved to London and in 1763 married a wealthy brewer, Henry Thrale.

They lived in Streatham, in the Borough of Lambeth, at a house built by Henry's father in the 1730s, demolished in 1863. It was very grand, and the Thrales entertained in style, being hosts to many of the literary and artistic leaders of the time, including (for instance) Sir Joshua Reynolds. Johnson was one of them, and it was as a result of his increasingly close friendship with Hester that he went on tour with the Thrales to her home country, in Denbighshire, in July to September, 1774.

When Henry Thrale died in 1781 Hester, in her early forties, fell in love with an Italian music teacher, Gabriel Piozzi, and, much to the displeasure of Dr. Johnson, married him. Perhaps because the marriage was not acceptable to London society she took him back to Tremeirchion, where she still had property. Here she built, and they lived in, the pleasant country mansion Bryn Bella, which still occupies a significant area on the outskirts of the village. Behind Bryn Bella's elegant gates lie substantial gardens.

Hester Piozzi died in 1821 and is buried here at Corpus Christi, together with her husband Gabriel Piozzi.

Tremeirchion's church is firmly placed at its centre, where (in spite of its rather loose and random spread into neighbouring countryside) the heart of the village undoubtedly is. There is the firm cluster of adjacent institutions: the school, the church, and the pub (hardly surprisingly The Salusbury Arms) which give to this village, as to several in the Vale, a rare identity in Welsh-village terms: that of the nucleated settlement.

Similarly nucleated (in terms of the proximity of the pub to the church) is the neighbouring village of **Bodfari**, which is said to have a Roman origin, the name coming from Varis, which may be related to the name of the Roman camp near St. Asaph, Varae. Roman coins and urns have been found there. Nothing Roman is apparent about it now, nor are its other main characteristics all that evident, since the iron age hillfort of Moel y Gaer is just outside the village but not immediately obvious, and the confluence of the rivers Clwyd and Wheeler which take place here does so in the valley bottom below Bodfari, beyond the Denbigh to Mold road which follows the Wheeler's course across the Clwyd valley, without any great sense of incidence.

Among Clwydian villages perhaps **Llandyrnog** is a paradigm, with its substantial double-aisled church and next-door pub, natural woodland with banks of wild flowers flanking the foothills above it which rise to the Clwydian range. Signs of a drovers' road on the approach tell us something about the place before we get there – those broad verges, hedges set well back, which evidence their ancient origins by the age, each side, of the hedgerow trees. Sure enough, in drovers village fashion, there are three pubs within this tiny community, and for once, uncharacteristically, Llandyrnog's means of survival now is evident, since it has on its outskirts a large creamery, now devoted to making cheese.

In the church at Llandyrnog, as also at the second church of this parish, **Llangwyfan**, are several memorials to members of the Madocks (or Maddocks) family, of which Mr. Wilson (in *Parish of Llandyrnog and Llangwyfan*) says with uncharac-

The Vale of Clwyd is renowned for its village inns,
as these two at Llandyrnog

Signs that this country road approaching Denbigh originated as a drovers'
road are the wide verges, and old hedgerow trees on either side prove that
this was its original form

Llanrhaeadr church and Jesse window

The almshouses at Llanrhaeadr

teristic vagueness 'whose ancestors apparently founded the towns of Porthmadog and Tremadog.' In fact these towns were founded by William Alexander Madocks, during the second and third decades of the 19th century, and he had no descendants with his name, only a daughter. Nevertheless there is an undoubted connection between the founder of Tremadog and Porthmadog and the area of Llandyrnog, since Madocks inherited some land here, in Denbighshire. It appears to have descended from his father, who however lived in Kent and took no notice of it, and indeed it did not contribute to William's eventual expensive schemes, since it was entailed to some cousins, so could not be sold, and eventually seems to have reverted to his eldest brother. But the land in the Llangwyfan area came to the family from their ancestors, the family, presumably, of both the Denbighshire and the Tremadog Madockses, since they were ultimately descended from a governor of Diserth Castle in the reign of Henry II.

The double-aisled church is recognised as a feature of the Vale. There are in all twenty one of these, (according to Peter L Wilson's little book, *Parish of Llandyrnog and Llangwyfan*) all built in the15th to 16th centuries. An outstanding example is the noble church of **Llanrhaeadr**, on the eastern bank of the Vale, famous for its Jesse Window, which bears the date of 1533. The term for it comes from its subject matter, the descent of Jesus from King David, son of Jesse.

The window is itself something of a hero, having survived the Civil War in hiding. Knowing that the Cromwellians destroyed stained glass windows the community of Llanrhaeadr took it out and hid it in the woods in an oak chest, replacing it on the Restoration. It has been cleaned by glaziers of York in the 1980s.

The tower of the church is 13th century although there has been a church here, of some sort, since St. Dyfnog founded one in the sixth century, the age of saints, near to the well which probably gave the parish its name; but the body of the present building is, like the other typical Clwydian churches, 15th century. Once again, a pub sits directly opposite, contributing to the focal nature of this spot (with the eighteenth-century almshouses still in place beyond the church) at the village's heart.

It must be said that the reason for the frequency of the double-aisled form in this area seems not to be known, since the author of the little booklet, *St. Dyfnog's Church*, gives six possible reasons, all of them hard to credit. We may think it sufficient to describe it as a local fashion, which blossomed for a time of significant prosperity (and hence of church building) during the years of Tudor government.

These villages are set at road junctions, but the junctions are of roads running across the valley with those running along its flanks. At **Llanbedr Dyffryn Clwyd** however we have a route across the hills themselves, as the road climbs twisting from between the large and successful pub and the church to curve around the base of Moel Eithinen, on its way from Ruthin to Mold. Llanbedr D.C. had a medieval church which was abandoned in 1862, the new one alongside the A494 being dedicated the next year. From above it,up the rare road across the hills, you get an overview of the Vale, miniaturised by distance and yet thick with detail.

Taking the road south from the other side of the ridge one comes down the valley of yet another river (the Alyn) into the country known as Iâl. This was a *cwmwd*, in the old local government structure, later, with the Norman system, becoming a lordship, in the gift of the king of Powys. It is transliterated into English as Yale, and in fact the Iâl family, whose seat of Plas yn Iâl lay to the west of the village, in the end called themselves Yale.

Some members of the family had emigrated to America, and it was there that Elihu Yale was born, in 1649. He came back with his father while still as infant, and eventually became a governor of the East India Company. When he came back from Madras he did so with an enormous fortune, and lived then in retirement partly in London and partly on his family's property in Denbighshire. When in the early 18th century Cotton Mather wished to set up a college at New Haven, he approached Yale as an old friend for financial assistance. Elihu sent, instead of

Llanbedr Dyffryn Clwyd

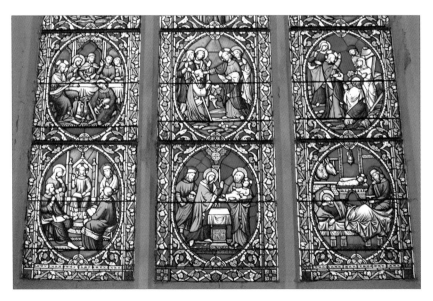

Details from the window in Llanbedr church

Llanarmon-yn-Iâl church

*St. Garmon
statue in the church*

Alms chest in the church

money, a large collection of books, pictures and furniture. These evidently sufficed to start the college, and by this rather indirect connection it came to be called after him, Yale University.

The other part of **Llanarmon**'s name is also of interest, since the dedication to St. Garmon makes it one of a clear set of such dedications spread evenly around Gwynedd and Powys. There are in fact nine of them, reaching from Llanarmon on the Llŷn peninsula to St. Harmons on the river Severn. Tradition associates this wandering saint with St. Germanus of Auxerre, Nennius, in the early ninth century, copied a Life of St. Germanus into his *Historia*. Here we read that Germanus came to Britain to preach and convert, and after several problematic meetings presided at the destruction of Vortigern, the High King. Bede fills out this account: Germanus was sent from Gaul, twice, in answer to a plea from the British church for someone to help them combat the heresy of Pelagianism.

It must be said that neither Nennius' nor Bede's account of Germanus' visits to Britain give any substance to the idea that he founded churches in northern Wales, and in fact the supposed connection of St. Garmon with the saint of Auxerre is now generally discounted.

Llanarmon was the traditional capital of the commote of Ial, and its ancientness is testified to by discovery of neolithic remains in a cave just east of the river Alyn, in which area, as if in defence of the river, the remains of a motte and bailey castle known as Tomen y Maerdre record its early medieval status. It did not however come into prominence again until it became a focus for several drovers' roads in the 19th century, and rose for a time on the prosperity given by cattle passage from Anglesey to England. Droving died out toward the end of that century, when cattle became more easily moved by railway,and for Llanarmon its limestone quarry (still evident on the west side of its valley) became its major employer. Now the village is noticeably restored, and has a self-confident and friendly air.

Chapter 3

DENBIGH

Denbigh's story comes in several phases, each of which has altered the town's identity and its position in relation to its neighbours. It was not, from the start, one of Edward's boroughs, the walled garrison towns which form such a clear imposed pattern in northern Wales. Indeed it appears to have been a native fortified settlement before we can even trace its recorded history, since the name means, in Welsh, 'small fort', *din bych*. We must suppose this small fort to have been on the rocky hill which subsequently became the site of the castle, since this rises so prominently above the wide flat valley that no-one building forts could resist fortifying it.

Even when it comes into history it does so not as the Norman stronghold which it was to become, but as a seat of the independent Welsh princes, even after the conquest, since Edward gave it to Dafydd, the problematic brother of Llywelyn, and before that, in 1269, Llywelyn himself had dated some letters from there as if it was one of his courts. It became Dafydd's by the terms of the Treaty of Conwy, in 1277, in recognition of his help to the Norman king; and when Dafydd characteristically changed sides again, in 1282, starting the final war by an attack on Hawarden, he withstood a siege there for a month that autumn.

It was only after things settled down a bit that Denbigh resumed some normal linear history, receiving its charter in 1290 and remaining the county town of the new shire (imposed by the Statute of Rhuddlan) until as late as 1888.

Denbigh's launch into history was initially guided by three Treaties, The Treaty of Woodstock in 1247, the Treaty of Montgomery in 1267, and the Treaty of Conwy (or Aberconway) in 1277. Woodstock was the implement by which Henry III (Edward I's father) took control of conquered lands in this area,

Denbigh castle

The Burgess Gate

Denbigh castle and details of perimeter walls

Llywelyn Fawr's stronghold at Tomen y Rhodwydd, Llanarmon-yn-Iâl

Dyffryn Clwyd and the other cantrefi, when Llywelyn ap Gruffydd made peace, under pressure, with Henry, after the death of Llywelyn the Great in 1240. This involved renouncing rights to the Perfedddwlad, and so destroyed the unity of Wales made by Llywelyn the Great and admitted the imposition on Wales of a feudal obligation. Henry had already taken for himself the earldom of Chester when the Earl John died childless in 1237, and this included the Perfeddwlad and adjoining lands in Powys. When he went to the continent in 1250 he left this considerable stretch of the border under the control of his son Edward, who came to Wales then 'to survey his castles and his lands in Gwynedd' for the first time, in 1256.

Llywelyn recovered those lands which had been lost, in 1256, but they were forfeited again in 1277 at the Treaty of Conwy and given to his brother Dafydd. He was dealing by then with Edward as king, but had it not been for the wayward behaviour of Dafydd the matter would have been patched up in a final form, with Henry still on the throne but Edward in control of Wales as 'Lord of the Crown Lands in Wales', when the Treaty of Montgomery gave certain lands and rights to Llywelyn in 1267. Henry was not in a position then to pursue the war against Llywelyn. He was short of money after the long dispute with his barons, led by Simon de Montfort, with whom Llywelyn had allied, before the former's death at Evesham in 1265. The treaty was arranged by the Papal legate, and it gave Llywelyn the right to the title Prince of Wales. He gained from Edward the four cantrefs of the Perfeddwlad and various overlordships through mid and south Wales. Edward kept the castles of Diserth and Deganwy, and the trouble emerged again when he succeeded as king, in 1272, and returned from crusade in 1274.

When Edward regained the fort at Denbigh from Dafydd this set the town on the route to its independent future, since he did not treat it in the same way as his other 'bastide' towns, but handed it to the commander of his Welsh campaign, Henry de Lacey, Earl of Lincoln. Not just the castle but the lordship of Denbigh were awarded to de Lacey, and to him fell the task of building the castle in its new form. Edward came himself to set in motion the undertaking, at the end of October, 1282, and he brought with him his master-mason, the virtuoso castle-builder James of St. George.

Because it was then left to de Lacey to build it, it never quite got finished. It is surmised that de Lacey lost heart after the death of his two sons. The eldest was said to have fallen down the well of Denbigh castle, though this is apparently hearsay, since Leland reports it as such. 'Sum say that the erle of Lincoln's sunne felle into the castle welle and ther dyed: whereupon he never passid to finish the castelle.' The second son fell off the battlements of his castle at Pontefract, while chasing a ball.

Like other such schemes the fortress was designed to house a colony, and burgages were established both within and outside the walls. The idea of a town was new to Wales, the nearest historical form being the civil settlements around the Roman camps. With 52 burgage plots inside the walls and 183 outside them the first town of Denbigh was definitely up on this hill. It did not, however, stay there all that long. For one thing a hilltop site is not the best for a rising market town, and gives rise inevitably to water problems. But what decided Denbigh to move down the hill was the experience of war. The castle may have been intended to protect the implanted population, but it came to be obvious that instead it represented a hazard to them. The town was burnt during the Wars of the Roses, in 1468, and was not rebuilt. A new town came into being down the hill.

There still remained some burgage plots within the walls, but many more were founded around the new market place. Some hundred years later (in 1586) Camden says:

The old town is now deserted and a new one, much larger, sprung up at the foot of the hill which is now so populous that the church not being large enough for the inhabitants, they have now begun to build a new one where the old town stood.

In other words by then the site of the old town within the walls

St Hilary's church

Leicester's church

St. Marcella's church

Sir John Salusbury (d. 1578) and wife, Joan

had been cleared, to become what now has the appearance of being the outer ward of the castle. The castle itself provided a handy quarry for the building of the new town, particularly after it fell out of military use at the end of the English Civil War. It was not until the mid 19th century that it came to be appreciated as historical ruins, and only then the town organised itself into protecting and securing the remnants.

The sprawling ruin is now largely invisible from the town, set back on its hill. There are some fine touches, such as the ornamented gatehouse, but even here one cannot avoid the feeling that it is incomplete. Perhaps most striking, because an example of overstatement, is the Burgess Gate, separate from the castle complex and looming over the town.

Henry de Lacey's rule over Denbigh was not a total success. In 1294, while the castle was still under construction, he had to deal with the revolt of Prince Madog. The rebels took the castle, and de Lacey's relieving force was defeated that November. Edward had to step in to rectify the situation, and in December he re-took Denbigh. The town suffered further in the usual conflicts, being burnt by the followers of Owain Glyndŵr in 1400, and largely destroyed, and transposed to the present market area, in the Wars of the Roses. Finally it became a Royalist refuge in the Civil War, in 1643, surrendered to the Parliamentarians in 1646, after which the castle became a ruin.

Perhaps the most significant thing to have happened to Denbigh during its historical biography was the gift of the town and lordshsip by Elizabeth I to Robert Dudley, Earl of Leicester. The county town and productive farmland which surrounded it contributed to the Earl's already plentiful wealth and importance. When Camden says, in 1586, that the townspeople were building a new church because the old one was too small for the expanding population, he perhaps refers to the ambitious project launched by Leicester with the aim of providing a Protestant alternative to St. Asaph cathedral. The old garrison church of St. Hilary which stood within the walls and amongst the burgages is represented now only by its prominent tower, the body of the church having been demolished in the 1920s. Leicester's church, begun in 1578, is nearby. It stands in the form of a long row of high arched windows, and the ruins of both failed churches, the Protestant and the Catholic, confront each other now across a stretch of vacant land, which was once the main part of the town.

It is said (by Thomas Pennant, writing in the18th century) that the reason Leicester did not succeed in completing his huge work is that the animosity felt to him throughout Wales made it hard to raise funds. Nevertheless the church seems to have been built enough tot be used, since its first vicar was William Morgan, the remarkable scholar who first translated the Bible into Welsh. It is perhaps hard to appreciate the courageous innovativeness of the concept now, of Leicester's church, the emphasis on clear light and plainness of form, the lack of decoration, the size, the placing, with its outlook over the Earl's lands.

Dudley managed to get so intensely disliked largely in his absence, since he seems to have spent his time putting on lavish entertainments at his seat of Kenilworth, and he could perhaps have blamed his agents for his bad press. He used the Sidney family to do his Welsh business (Sir Henry, President of the Council for Wales, was his brother-in-law) and on the spot in Denbigh were the Middletons. They had been at Gwaenynog Hall, to the west of the town, above the river Ystrad, since the reign of Richard III. Three generations of them held the post of Governor of Denbigh Castle, and during the third generation of these Sir Thomas Middleton owned lands in Meirionydd and Lincolnshire, and practised as a money-lender; in 1595 he bought Chirk Castle and its lordship. He was active in business in England, being among other things a founder shareholder of the East India Company, and in 1613 became Lord Mayor of London. His son, also Thomas, bought Ruthin castle.

It is not surprising that several times in history the Middleton family found itself in dispute with the Salusburys, who remained in place at Lleweni. Both families are commemorated in St. Marcella's, Denbigh's Parish Church. Called Whitchurch, and traditionally a landmark for travellers because of its whitewashed

The old cross and medieval stocks near the Guildhall, Denbigh

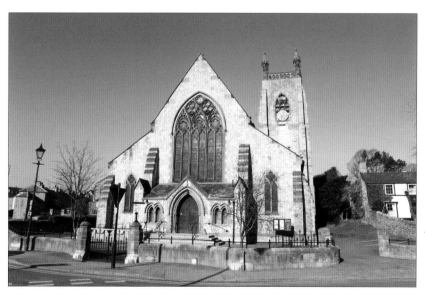

The church now stands at Pwllygrawys – the 'pool of Lent' – once the location of the fish pond used by the old priory during religous abstentions

33

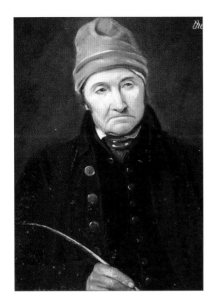 

Twm o'r Nant   *Twm o'r Nant's grave*
                        at St. Marcella's

Theatr Twm o'r Nant – Twm's dramatic tradition lives on

walls, it is dedicated to St. Marccella, a saint perhaps called Marchell (since the church is also known as Llanfarchell), who supposedly founded it in the sixth century. Its origins in that age gain plausibility from its location: now white again, on its own on a little hill, like other churches and churchyards which have grown around the original cells of early eremitic 'saints' it is surprisingly distant from any settlement.

St. Marcella's fell into disrepair in the late 19th century, Denbigh's other churches (St. Mary's, built in 1874, and St. David's, rebuilt in 1894, which has a window by Burne Jones) being in more popular use. Now restored, it has become again the recognised Parish Church of the town. Doubled-aisled, in the Clwyd fashion, it has two magnificent 15th century hammer-beam roofs, and at the east end of one aisle the superb double alabaster-effigy tomb of Sir John Salusbury, who died in 1578, and his wife Joan. The Middleton family (sometimes, as here, spelt Myddleton) is represented by a brass monument on the north wall, originally in the porch, which commemorates Sir Richard, one of the governors of Denbigh Castle,whose son Thomas became Lord Mayor of London. In the churchyard is the grave of Twm o'r Nant, the Welsh poet (Thomas Edwards), born in 1738, who developed from an uneducated farmboy to become a popular writer of ballads and of interludes, which have given him a significant place in the history of Welsh literature.

While the Myddletons still lived at Gwaenynog, in the 18th century, they received a visit which evidently gratified them, since Colonel John set up a memorial to commemorate it, which states:

This spot was often dignified by the presence of Samuel Johnson LL.D., whose moral writings, exactly conformable to the precepts of Christianity, gave ardour to Virtue and confidence to Truth.

Johnson himself was appalled by the idea: it looked, he said, 'like an intention to bury me alive'.

His own recollection of the visit seems greatly less significant. 'I dined at Mr. Myddleton's, of Gwaenynog', he writes in his diary. 'After dinner, the talk was of preserving the Welsh language... Myddleton is the only man who, in Wales, has talked to me of literature.'

Dr. Johnson was by then, by 1774, already famous. For one thing, his monumental work, *A Dictionary of the English Language*, had been published in 1755, and its popularity was such that it went through five editions in his lifetime. Overshadowed by this achievement his other books are now forgotten, but he gained some prominence as a literary critic and producer of literary magazines.

Johnson's connections with Denbigh are clear but restricted, and it would be be as well to dispel the popular idea that he came to visit Mrs. Thrale. She had not lived in Wales for a considerable time, having gone to London when her father's financial situation ran into trouble, married Thrale in London, and lived with him at Steatham and Southwark, in London. She did not return to live in Wales until her husband died, when she married Mr. Piozzi and built Bryn Bella. Johnson first met the Thrales through the agency of a Mr. Murphy, who (Boswell says) was intimate with Mrs. Thrale and had 'spoken very highly of Dr. Johnson'. The Thrales and Johnson got on so well that 'he became one of the family, and an apartment was appropriated to him both in their house at Southwark and in their villa at Streatham.'

It was, however, with the Thrales that he set out on a tour to north-east Wales, and it was because of her property there, where some business had to be settled, that the trip took place:

I have just begun to print my Journey to the Hebrides, and am leaving the press to take another journey into Wales, whither Mr.Thrale is going to take possession of, at least, five hundred a year, fallen to his lady.

The duration of the trip is clear; he wrote to Boswell on July 4th, 1774, 'I am going into Wales to-morrow'; and to Boswell again on

The Johnson memorial by a ford on river Ystrad
– one of his favourite locations

Gwaenynog Hall

Gwaenynog and its secret Beatrix Potter garden

The Guildhall and Guildhall Tavern – the Old Bull Hotel

1st October 'Yesterday returned from my Welsh journey'.

While he was there he took the opportunity to see 'a new part of the island'. He went to the cathedral towns of St. Asaph and Bangor, the mountains of Penmaenmawr and Snowdon, and crossed to Anglesey, in all, as he said, visiting five of the six counties of North Wales. Evidently the Thrale party were based at Lleweni, staying with the Salusburys (her relatives), since Johnson writes a letter from there on 16th August, saying 'Mr. Thrale's affairs have kept him here a great while, nor do I know exactly when we shall hence'. Boswell also is surprised: 'Wales has probably detained you longer than I supposed.' He comments that Johnson 'will have become quite a mountaineer, by visiting Scotland one year and Wales another' and hopes some literature will result: 'Cambria will complain if you do not honour her with some remarks'. But Johnson does not write anything about Wales, and Boswell says did not keep any notes or journal (though he did, as we have seen, keep a diary) which neglect was because (the Doctor says) 'Wales is so little different from England, that it offers nothing to the speculation of the traveller'. He had expected 'bleak and barren mountains' but found only 'green and fertile ones', suggesting that he had seen much more of the Vale of Clwyd than of Snowdonia. Boswell's disappointment is the strongest implication that this was the only time the great man came to Wales.

Gwaenynog, the ancient home of the Myddletons, now a substantial rural property set in the lush pastures of dairy-land, is the site also of another famous visit. It is now owned by the great-great-niece of Beatrix Potter, Mrs. Janie Smith, and it is said that Potter came there 'more than a dozen times' between 1895 and 1913, when it was owned by her uncle, Fred Burton. The garden there, now restored to its form at that time, is traditionally the inspiration for the rabbit theme and the setting of *The Tale of the Flopsy Bunnies*, and its illustrations.

Born in Kensington in 1866, Potter spent family childhood holidays at seaside resorts in the south of England, which later provided settings for some of her books, and eventually she became mainly associated with the Lake District, where she bred sheep at Hill Top Farm, Sawrey, near Ambleside. The Flopsy Bunny book was published in 1909, when she was 36. In the book there are pictures of various rabbits, and four of a garden with a path with box-hedge edgings, sprawling perennials and decorative arches. In one of these sketches the gable end of a building can be glimpsed, with a gothic style window, intended as a view of Mr. McGregor's house, which is of the same form as the two-storey pottingshed at Gwaenynog. There also exists a fine watercolour painted by Potter in May 1912 of a view from above Gwaenynyog. Very pleasing and idyllic, it now belongs to the Free Library of Philadelphia.

There are still rabbits in the garden at Gwaenynog, though it is not known whether they are more whimsical and anthropomorphic than rabbits elsewhere.

Besides these visitors Denbigh, in its long history, has been the birthplace of several eminent people. The birth, in 1841, in a cottage under the castle on the back side, away from the town, of a son to an unmarried couple, who took his father's surname of Rowlands, could hardly have been less propitious. He only became Henry Morton Stanley, the great Victorian-period explorer, some time later, and after several unexpected turns of fate. The cottage, near the Great Gateway, was demolished in the 1890s.

John Rowlands, as he still was, had some way to go before he found fame. The illegitimate child was brought up by his grandfather and then, when he died, some other relatives, but his childhood ended in the workhouse at St. Asaph, which in modern times became the H. M. Stanley hospital, but has now closed.

He was 18 when he set out to find, rather literally, a new life. He enlisted on a trans-Atlantic voyage, jumped ship in New Orleans, and there was befriended by a successful merchant, Henry Hope Stanley, whose surname he then took. There he became in all respects American, even to the extent of serving in the Civil War, first with the Confederates and then for the Unionists. He joined the Union Navy in 1864, but again jumped

Denbigh remains the market town for local produce and culture

Denbigh town pubs

H. M. Stanley   *David Livingstone*

The controversial Stanley statue

ship, this time in New Hampshire. It was, evidently, a land of opportunity, since without much training he then became a journalist and graduated to become a foreign correspondent for the newly-formed New York Herald. It was as such, with some persuasion on his part, than he was put in charge of an expedition to find Dr.Livingstone. The famous Scottish missionary had been missing in Africa for some time.

The trip was arduous at the time, and strangely remains problematic to this day. Many people were against the erection of a statue to Stanley in the centre of Denbigh since he has, increasingly, gained a reputation for colonial exploitation. He had two hundred porters – the Herald had given him an open budget – and became notorious for treating them badly. It was, apparently, his contemporary Victorian explorer Sir Richard Burton who said: 'Stanley shoots negroes as if they were monkeys'. The expedition through 700 miles of tropical jungle led to a lot of losses, starting with Stanley's own horse, which was bitten by a tsetse fly. However they reached Ujiji, near Lake Tanganyika, in November 1871, some seven months after they had set off from Zanzibar.

The second controversial point is whether he ever uttered the banality which, more than anything, has made him famous. Rather more unfortunate than the possible celebration of a lapse of human rights is the fact that the instigators of the statue have chosen to perpetuate the dubious cliche as the essence of what was probably a great man. The statue demeans its subject by showing him in the act of greeting Livingstone, inevitably encouraging children to play at being Livingstone by shaking his hand.

Livingstone did not use the words when recalling the meeting. Stanley removed from his own diary the page relating to the moment. The Herald itself, publishing its account of the occasion the next summer, says:

Preserving a calmness of exterior before the Arabs which was hard to simulate as he reached the group, Mr. Stanley said –

'Doctor Livingstone, I presume?' A smile lit up the features of the hale white man as he answered: 'Yes, and I feel thankful that I am here to welcome you.'

The cynical now surmise that the explorer himself later made the details up.

Stanley had many more adventures in Africa, though it is inevitable that he will be remembered for that one meeting at Ujiji. Although some of his work resulted in the commandeering of the Congo by the Belgians, he was knighted in 1899 for his services to the British Empire.

Less honoured, and the subject of a less dramatic life, an eminent contemporary of Stanley's hardly left Denbigh at all. Thomas Gee, born in Denbigh in 1815, was apprenticed in his father's printing works, which he in due course took over in 1838. From 1845 he became engaged there in serious publishing. A Methodist and a Liberal, he specialised in Welsh language works, and his press was a significant force in keeping alive the language which was then very much under threat. In particular his newspaper, *Baner ac Amserau Cymru*, was a rare vehicle for Welsh news and opinions.

When he died, in 1898, the publishing business was carried on by his son, and it remained in the family until 1914. The works, at the bottom of town, closed in 2001, and the impressively functional building in which they were housed had already started to fall into disrepair. A local preservation trust has been formed and taken on the historical site, with the intention of converting it into a community facility and 'museum of printing', displaying and interpreting its remarkable heritage.

Denbigh retains its past without being encumbered by it. Although the inevitable supermarkets loom at its edges, its town centre is busy with real shops. It clearly has assets other than visitors to sustain it. It lives comfortably with its considerable history.

Thomas Gee

The old Gee printing works – there are dreams of a heritage centre

Capel Mawr, Denbigh, where Thomas Gee was a leading deacon

Ruthin town square

*Ruthin was a centre for drovers travelling from western Wales
to the English markets*

Chapter 4

RUTHIN

The road into Ruthin is recognisable as a drove road even before you get to the Drovers' Arms. The drovers met each other at Ruthin Fair where cattle were sold every Monday. They went on from here via Wrexham to the Shropshire markets. Part of Ruthin's function was this service at the interface, a punctuation on the road to England.

Part of of its historical purpose, along with that of Denbigh, also lay in its corresponding role the other way – the way into Wales. Both towns, when fortified, served as protections of the lines of supply, and of retreat, for any army manoeuvring in this direction, across the border from the Cheshire plain. So it was that in 1277 the Justiciar of Chester, a Marcher Lord called Reginald de Grey, was given by the king the right and obligation of building a castle to defend Ruthin on his behalf.

Grey built the castle in the early 1280's, and after Edward himself had inspected the works, coming over from Denbigh in October 1282, the incipient castle and the cantref of Dyffryn Clwyd were handed over to him as a personal fiefdom, which then descended in his family for several generations.

So it was that some hundred and twenty years later the third baron, another Reginald, became almost by accident the immediate cause of the great outbreak of national fervour, the uprising of Owain Glyndŵr. This was on the face of it surprising, since Owain, with Norman as well as Welsh ancestry, and owner of land on the English border, was of much the same background as Grey. The two men had known each other since their youth, having been companions in arms in the retinue of the Earl of Arundel, in France, in 1387. But circumstances placed them on opposite sides of a growing conflict when Henry Bolingbroke usurped the throne of England by the overthrow of Richard II.

The quarrel between Glyndŵr and Grey has all the appearance of being a set-up designed to settle old competition, perhaps of something as elusive as status. There was a dispute over a piece of land, but this is hardly surprising or unusual. More significant, perhaps, was what appears to have been an outright attempt on Grey's part to discredit Glyndŵr. He was entrusted with the summons which Henry IV issued for Glyndŵr to attend the Scottish war. Failing to deliver it until it was too late he then represented Owain to the king as a traitor, and succeeded in getting him outlawed. It is hardly surprising then that the first act of the war for independence was a strikingly personal attack by Glyndŵr on Grey.

The 18th of September, 1400, was a Saturday, and in Ruthin it was shortly before the St. Matthew's Day fair. Glyndŵr arrived with a troop from his court at Glyndyfrdwy and they burnt the town. Grey himself, however, remained impregnable within his castle, and it was not until 1402, when he attacked Ruthin again, that Glyndŵr finally got the better of Grey, luring him into a trap near his castle at Ruthin and taking him captive. Ruthin castle was acquired from the Greys by the crown in the reign of Henry VII, and in due course sold by Charles I to Thomas Myddleton, whose main seat then was at Chirk. When the Civil War broke out it was commandeered by the crown again, and Myddleton found himself leading a Parliamentary force against his own home.

General Mytton was called in to complete the work, but so effective was the defensive structure that the royalists in the castle held out for an eleven week siege. When they finally surrendered the castle was systematically demolished, from 1648, and the stones used over the years to supply Ruthin with building stone and finally to construct, on the ancient site, what is now the Ruthin Castle Hotel.

Famous though this institution is, it cannot compare, in social folklore, with the high period of the same building's prime, the time when the future Edward VII was Prince of Wales. Maria, the daughter of the last Myddleton owner, married the younger son of John West, Lord de la Warr, and their son Frederick married

Owain Glyndŵr's Day – 16th September – and his attack on colonial Ruthin being celebrated in the town

Ruthin Castle and Hotel

the ward and heiress of Admiral Cornwallis, with the result of bequeathing to Ruthin castle its association with the family of Cornwallis-West.

William Cornwallis-West, who inherited this complicated background and the fortune that went with it, lived in Ruthin Castle during the last decades of the Victorian era and the years leading up to the Great War. He was Lord Lieutenant of Denbighshire from 1872 till his death in 1917, and Member of Parliament for Denbighshire from 1885 to 1892. In that year he added to his status by marrying a noted Irish beauty and hostess, Mary Fitzpatrick, with whom he established a social scene at Ruthin Castle which contrasts strikingly with the solid yeoman respectability of the town.

This evidently flamboyant and perhaps even daring set-up attracted the participation of the Prince of Wales, who called it 'the Wild West Show'. One term which undoubtedly describes this Ruthin Castle household is 'well-connected'. One of their daughters became Princess of Pless and a second married the Duke of Westminster. Their son George in due course became the second husband of Winston Churchill's mother, Lady Randolph Churchill. But the moral is that such excesses are not durable: George, the son, got himself and the property into vast debt, and in spite of this (or possibly because of it) he married for the second time, in 1914, the vastly successful star actress known (from her first marriage) as Mrs. Patrick Campbell, whose first husband had died in the Boer War in 1900. Beatrice Tanner, as she was born, had a stage career which boomed in America from 1900, and among her many notable successes was the main role in Shaw's Pygmalion, in the year she married West, which Shaw had written specially for her. She took it to New York with great success in 1915.

Ruthin Castle itself then edged out of history slowly, being, between the wars, an exclusive clinic, and from the 1960's a hotel.

Contemporary in its origins with the castle, at the start of the town of Ruthin, and still very much at its heart, is St. Peter's church, secluded from the town surrounding it by its protective mature trees. The dedication itself proclaims it as Norman; the older Celtic church at Llanrhydd, a little to the south-east of the town (in keeping with the tendency of early Welsh churches to follow their founding saint's preference for being apart from population settlements), was dedicated to the local saint, Meugan. Peter, like Mary, was a popular dedication in Norman times, and their influence along the border can be plotted by the occurrence of these saints in church names.

St. Peter's was founded by Reginald de Grey, in the reign of Edward I. It was founded as a collegiate church, and described in the Taxatio of Lincoln in 1291 as a 'flourishing collegiate establishment'. Under the lordship of Reginald's son John de Grey it became an amalgamation of parish church and collegiate. The difference is that a collegiate church has, as the name implies, an educational function, and is constructed to house a body of canons and presbyteries. Though the structure connected with this may be seen, in the form of the old Ruthin grammar school and the cloisters connected with the college of priests, this function was curtailed when all such institutions were dissolved by Henry VIII, in his curtailment of monastic influence between 1536 and 1539.

The decline in the fortunes of the Greys began a little earlier, since the family had never recovered financially from the hefty ransom paid to Glyndŵr, and in 1508 the 4th baron sold the lordship of Ruthin to Henry VII. It is supposed that the magnificent panelled roof of the north nave was a gift from Henry. However, this is unlikely, since some of the families commemorated by their coats of arms on the panels had fallen out of royal favour by then. This makes the date of the great ceiling even earlier, and its more modest companion over the south nave is also of Tudor period, probably late 16th century. Incidentally St. Peter's is perhaps the prototype of the Vale of Clwyd style of double naved churches, said (in this case) to have been initiated by Archbishop John Peckham, of the early years of the conquest, who wished to separate the canons from the laity. So opines Keith Kenyon-Thompson, in his book *Rhuthin*; but

St. Meugan's church, Ruthin

St. Peter's churchyard gates

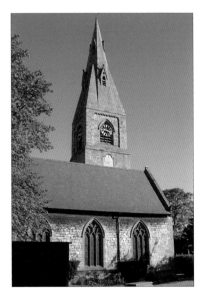

St. Peter's church, Ruthin

The new Craft Centre at Ruthin

The Barclays bank building at Ruthin town square

unfortunately this must be wrong, since the south nave was not added until the second half of the 14th century, some hundred years after Peckham. The church's own guide book attributes it to a growth in population at that time.

The church informs us, as parish churches do, of the people who were important to the community over its long period. Memorials to the Goodman family recognise that it was Dean Gabriel Goodman who revived the church during the late 16th century. Goodman, though born in Ruthin in 1528, became famous as Dean of Westminster and influential in the early years of Anglicanism. He was one of the signatories, for instance, to the Thirty-Nine Articles, and contributed to the translation known as The Bishops' Bible. Prominent at Court in the reign of Elizabeth, he went on to use his position to establish educational institutions, some in London, and here in Ruthin he founded Christ's Hospital and refounded Ruthin School.

It is impossible to go into or out of St. Peter's churchyard without being impressed by one of its major assets. In 1720 the Myddleton family of Chirk Castle, who were Lords of the Manor of Ruthin, paid the Davies brothers of Bersham, near Wrexham, £28.18.1d for designing and constructing the gates to the church, which were erected at the further expense of £20 in 1727.

The business had been founded by Huw Davies, who died in 1702, but it was brought into prominence by his four sons, Robert, John, Huw and Thomas – although it is the first two who are normally meant when people speak of the Davies Brothers, and it was in particular Robert who gained fame for design as well as engineering skill. He it was who was reputed to have trained under the French wrought-iron designer Jean Tijou, who in turn may have been trained at Verseilles. Certainly it is possible to see a line of stylistic influence running from the French to the English to the Welsh in this manner of baroque ironwork. Tijou, as a Huguenot, seems to have taken refuge in the Netherlands, and probably came to England with William and Mary in 1689, when he worked on the gates of Hampton Court, which they made their seat. He also became a colleague of Sir

Christopher Wren and was responsible for some ironwork at St. Paul's cathedral. The Davies Brothers have famous gates at Chirk Castle, which, being built in 1719, explain the choice of blacksmith commissioned here by Myddleton in 1720.

You move, through St. Peter's gates, not into the modern world but into one progressively matured over several hundred years and rich with the amalgamation of its several epochs. Chronologically this process starts a very long time ago, in the world of myth rather than history, since the oldest thing in St. Peter's Square is a large lump of limestone, which Kenyon-Thompson says was probably originally 'once a waymarker on a watershed'. It is called Maen Huail and the story connects it with King Arthur.

Huail, also called Heuil, was (significantly as it turns out) the brother of the historian Gildas, whose family came from the Pictish country which became Scotland. He occurs in early Welsh documents, such as *The Triads of Britain*, where he gets a brief mention, and the Mabinogion tale of *Culhwch and Olwen*, an early story in which he appears in a long list of the sons of Caw. The story of his connection with King Arthur is not mentioned in the text, but Lady Charlotte Guest traces it to a Welsh manuscript of 1611 copied by Edward Llwyd. In fact it appears to have been recorded earlier, in 1530, by Elis Gruffydd, who was born in Flintshire and became a soldier in the British army at Calais, and also a noted chronicler and translator. Briefly, the story says that Arthur and Huail were rivals for the affections of a certain lady, that a duel took place in which Arthur was wounded in the thigh, reconciliation agreed on condition that Huail should never mention the wound, from which Arthur continued to limp; years later, in Ruthin, Arthur is dancing in disguise when Huail is overheard to remark that the dancing was good apart from the limp, which Arthur took to be a breach of the agreement. He had Huail beheaded on a convenient stone 'which' (Lady Charlotte says) 'lay in the street of the town... This stone is still to be seen in the town of Rhuthyn.'

It is indeed, now tucked into a corner of the front of the

Maen Huail at the square in Ruthin

The plaque near Maen Huail

The old courthouse

The Dutch-influenced Myddleton Arms

Barclays Bank building, a large rough block which can scarcely have got into Ruthin's main square by mistake, and must have had a purpose there even before it became Huail's execution block.

The interesting feature of this fanciful little tale is that whatever lies behind it might provide the explanation for something which has always bothered historians. Gildas, though dealing in some detail with the period when Arthur was supposed to have existed, never mentions him. Because our early history is largely based on the work of Bede, and Bede copied Gildas, Arthur failed to get into conventional history, and remains caught in the world of myth. If there had been a quarrel between Arthur and Gildas, as there would have been if Arthur killed Gildas's brother, the discrepancy might be explained. Gildas attributed to someone else the achievements of which, it is elsewhere hinted, Arthur was the hero.

There are other sharp reminders of a varied and colourful past around the square. Another bank is housed in the old courthouse, a fine half-timbered structure built in 1401 because an even older one on this spot was burnt by Glyndŵr in 1400, at the start of his battle for Wales' independence, the first flame of a fire in Wales which has never quite gone out. Across the road the Castle Hotel contains some timber-work which escaped the fire, though the building's facade is splendidly Georgian and evocative of a prosperous time, and it itself adjoins another remarkable building, the Dutch-influenced Myddleton Arms, its seven dormer windows dominating its roof.

Traditionally Ruthin was divided into a Welsh and an English area (though the separation is not apparent now), the English section being under the walls of the castle, in Castle Street and Dog Lane. This is where the magnificent Nantclwyd House is, together with some other fine buildings, on the approach to the Castle gateway. The Welsh area apparently ran from Well Street in an arc as far as Mwrog Street. In Well Street is an old inn, the Wynnstay Arms, where George Borrow stayed briefly: 'Ruthyn is a dull town', he said, but of interest to him through its connection with Glyndŵr, a hero of his.

Nantclwyd House, the grounds of which back onto those of the Ruthin Castle Hotel, has a long and well-recorded history. Modern dating establishes its beginnings in the 1430s. It passed through years of ownership by largely professional people, until coming by marriage into the Thelwall family, in the mid 17th century. During this period, after much alteration over the years, it reached largely its present form. In due course it became the town house of the Wynnes of Coed Coch, Betws-yn-Rhos. Since then it has been in many varied uses – a school, a rectory, the home of the mayor – and was sold to the County Council in1984, after which, in modern times, it served as the visiting assize judges' lodgings.

Nantclwyd House is recognised as the oldest timber-framed house in Wales. Now painstakingly restored, it is displayed in a series of tableaux representing, room by room, seven periods of its use: the 1430s, Thelwall's occupation in 1690, an 1891 schoolroom, the 1916 rector's study, and finally (where you actually start) a hall laid out as 1942. The garden, meanwhile, is not so themed, and has a simple ancient atmosphere of comfortable times.

Ruthin's other notable building is its gaol, also now on show. This is a 19th century replacement of earlier inadequate houses of correction, and it owes its imposing character to the fact that it was based in style on Pentonville Prison. It remained in use for its original purpose until 1916. Since then it has been a library and an archive store, and still houses county records and is now restored to its Victorian character and a popular tourist facility.

Such eagerness to display its plentiful past is typical of the positive approach which epitomises Ruthin, confident of its status as a regional centre through its long period as the County Town of Denbighshire, interrupted when that county was replaced by the invented administrative area of Clwyd from 1974-6, when Mold (now in Flintshre) was the County Town. The Denbighshire County Council offices and the Town Hall still proclaim its habitual status in Market Street, at the bottom of which, beyond the roundabout, is the complex formed by the

Nantclwyd House

Ruthin gaol

61

Inside Ruthin gaol

*Loggerheads Country Park – with the Clwydian Range Centre
and Caffi Florence, nestling in the Clwydian Hills*

Craft Centre, an up-to-date exercise in the display of local skill and enterprise.

Through the gap in the Clwydian Hills to the east of Ruthin is the popular **Loggerheads Country Park**, an outdoor and walking centre with many amenities. Out of Ruthin southwards the roads rise from the Vale, the A494 following the Clwyd out of its plain and into the woodland slopes of a narrowed and more constrained landscape, more intimate than its broad flat extravagance of parkland and hedgerow trees. The two keep close company along with the route of the former railway until **Bryn Saith Marchog**, the hill of the seven knights. This strange name for a tiny hamlet is a literary reference which must have some authentic background.

When Brân, the king of Britain, left for Ireland, in the Mabinogion tale of *Branwen, daughter of Llŷr,* he left behind seven men to rule the island of Britain – *seith marchawc,* in antiquated Welsh – whom he left, the tale says, *yn edeirnon,* that is in the vale of Edeirnion, which actually lies a bit to the south of here. 'And because of that the name Saith Marchog was given to to the town.' There seem to be the beginnings of another story here (which perhaps once explained this precise location) but apart from a brief reference later in the tale of Branwen it has not survived.

Right next to Bryn Saith Marchog is what is perhaps the top village in the river's valley, **Derwen**, remarkable for its late-15th-century Celtic cross in the churchyard, and the grand arch-braced beamed roof of the church's interior. Dedicated to St. Mary, it has evidently post-conquest origins, and a single-naved unClwydian form. Particularly because it clearly portrays some grandeur, it is sad to find it now disused, cared for by the Friends of Friendless Churches.

By the time we reach **Gwyddelwern** the road has left the river, and reached a watershed between two major valleys, the Clwyd and the Dee, and between two sections of this book. Here we look forward, literally, to a much more sharply riven landscape. Wern means a swampy area, *gwyddel* a patch of thicket, so the name is purely descriptive (nothing to do with Irish as the prefix *Gwyddel* might imply). Here the church is dedicated to St. Beuno, an early wandering saint who had much influence both here and further west, and the circular form of its churchyard is said to indicate a pre-Christian site, perhaps the church being built within a stone circle. The graveyard has in this case been severely tidied up, straight rows of regimented graves allowing for easier mowing, and an ancient yew tree survives encumbered by a wall up its base. The church itself is out of use and showing signs of disrepair now, though it looks surprisingly English in a spired and perpendicular windowed way.

Gwyddelwern church

Derwen church and old cross in St. Mary's churchyard,
and detail of the head of the cross

Rhug Organic Farm Shop, grill and information centre near Corwen

Remains of the old cross in Corwen's churchyard

66

Chapter 5

VALLEY OF THE WATER OF THE DEE

When the river Dee flows out of Bala lake it runs through a valley called the Vale of Edeirnion (or Edeyrnion) which culminates at Corwen, after which it becomes the Vale of Llangollen. The area is traditionally called after Edeyrn, one of the sons of Cunedda, who, like his brother Meirion, gave his name to a district which he presumably ruled over. Here the Dee and the A5 become inseparable, both being where they are because constrained by the same geological fault.

Corwen was always a strategic location, standing on a river crossing between the kingdoms of Gwynedd and Powys. Here on the meadows of the old Rhug estate, Gruffudd ap Cynan – the fiery king of north-western Wales – was taken prisoner by the Normans during what was supposed to be a peace conference in the 12th century. Later, the town became a posting point since travellers came this way from Shrewsbury long before Telford built the improved road, but its history in this capacity received a radical boost from Telford's decision to route one of the major means of access to Wales through this valley, the Shrewsbury to Conwy route replacing to a large extent the old Irish road via Denbigh. Telford stated his intention, in April 1811, to build a road

> *from the English plains, where the river Dee leaves the mountains, at the bottom of the valley of Llangollen, and from thence to ascend along the south side of that river to the town of Corwen...*

He must have been guided to some extent by the fact that people were already going that way. John Byng, for instance, otherwise Viscount Torrington, wrote of his *Tour into North Wales* in 1793 that the road between Llangollen and Corwen was then 'steep and strong, but now widening and mending every day'. At Corwen he went to what was then the New Inn, now the Owain Glyndŵr Hotel. He is much taken with the scenery, impressed by the universal use of the Welsh language, but says little of the town. Perhaps this is just as well. The Reverend Bingley, a few years later, states tersely that Corwen 'is a disagreeable little town'. George Borrow, who came in the 1850's, and so after the A5 had been completed, also went to the Owain Glyndŵr inn (as it was by then) and had a drink, on his way to Cerrigydrudion, but disappointingly does not comment on the town.

The Owain Glyndŵr Hotel, formerly the New Inn, still forms a prominent feature of the town's centre. It bears a plaque at its entrance claiming to have been the location of the first eisteddfod 'to which the public were admitted' (the earlier version being apparently restricted to the competitors and judges) on 12th May 1789, an event which formed the prototype of the present form of eisteddfod, and was due to the persistance of a local man, Thomas Jones. It was a few years before Iolo Morganwg launched the idea on the world by the formation of the Gorsedd of Bards, in London in 1792.

Just behind the hotel lies the church, notable for signs of its antiquity, such as the pillar built into its entrance porch which is probably a pre-Christian standing stone, and for its dedication to saints Mael and Sulien, undoubtedly early Celtic missionaries. A medieval 'preaching cross' stands in the churchyard, 'a strange old pillar about a thousand years old', writes John Cowper Powys, in his *Obstinate Cymric*. Powys lived in Corwen with his partner Phyllis Playter from 1935 to 1955 (when they moved to Blaenau Ffestiniog), and here he wrote two novels: *Porius* and *Owen Glendower*.

You could not anyway ignore Glyndŵr in this region, but in Corwen's central square he dominates the view, fierce on his rearing charger, carrying forward to an endless future the unequivocal ideals of Wales.

Owain ap Gruffudd Fychan was born in about 1359 near here,

Corwen square, proudly paying hommage to Owain Glyndŵr

Owain Glyndŵr's Mount near Glyndyfrdwy

The river Dee below the Mount　　　*Owain Glyndŵr Hotel, Corwen*

on his father's estate in the Dee valley, from which he later took his surname. Lord of Glyndyfrdwy, he simplified the name of this lordship to Glyn Dŵr. **Glyndyfrdwy**, now a hamlet midway between Corwen and Llangollen, has a medieval motte, known as Owain Glyndŵr's Mount, which, though very prominent, lying close to the road, was actually not the site of his dwelling. Below it in the field is a hollow thought to have been the location of the moated manor which was his family home, probably his birthplace, though he lived in maturity mainly at Sycharth, nearer to the English border. The little tree-topped motte on a steep bank above the Dee, the track of the railway running cramped on its riverside slope and the A5 close on its other flank, was built by somebody else, presumably an Earl of Chester, to command the passage of this broad valley. It was here, at his Dee residence, that Owain was proclaimed Prince of Wales, on 16th September,1400.

The name, Glyndyfrdwy, is at the same time easily explained and partly inexplicable. The river Dee, known to the Romans as Deva, like the city called after it, is Afon Dyfrdwy in Welsh, and since the dyfr part of that means 'water' the 'dwy' is the distinguishing name – the water of the Dee – which remains unexplained any further. 'Dwy' apparently does not here mean 'two', as it might elsewhere. Perhaps it comes from the name of a distant river goddess; or perhaps not.

Following the proclamation came the war, and we have already seen some aspects of this, in Ruthin, for instance, where he carried out his first attack. A few years later the rebellion was becoming a serious problem to the English king. By 1403 the rival English Prince of Wales, later to become Henry V, was in charge of the king's forces in Wales, then aged sixteen. Though Shakespeare is often surprisingly accurate in his historical interpretation, we can, I think, discount as theatrical contrivance the goings on at the Boar's Head in Eastcheap. This was a serious prince, who became a serious king. The young Henry wrote to his father proudly from Shrewsbury that he had burnt Sycharth to the ground and then gone on to 'Glyndourdy'. There he burnt

Glyndŵr's other dwelling, his lodge, and destroyed his park and laid waste the surrounding country. It is as a result of this diligence, no doubt, that there is nothing to see there now of the great rebel's home.

Alongside the A5 today, either side, lie old stone walls. At least some of these were built to Telford's specifications when he designed the road. In some places two hundred years of raising the road level have reduced them to a few inches above ground, but they are recognisably Telford's, characterised by the upright layer of stones on top, forming a coping. What is remarkable is that in some places Telford walls survive both sides of the road, meaning that it is now still its original width. We may see then that this was for its time a major motorway, when traffic was scarce and it can hardly have been essential to allow two vehicles to pass. Since it suffices today we may see that Telford anticipated a change in circumstances to the present increase in use which he can hardly have had justification for at the time.

A route from Shrewsbury via Llangollen to the Conwy crossing had been in existence for some time, being first noted in 1776, but it was probably the extension of Lord Penrhyn's turnpike to Capel Curig, by an Act of Parliament in 1802, which implicitly laid out this route. Following the Act of Union between Britain and Ireland in 1800 the matter was brought before a House of Commons Committee by the Irish Chancellor of the Exchequer in 1810, since the road between London and Dublin, now frequently used by Irish Members of Parliament, was still inferior in its Welsh section to the stretches through the Midlands. Telford was working on roads in the Scottish highlands when he was appointed by the Commons Committee to make a survey of this stretch of road. He reported in April 1811, but it was not until 1815 that Sir Henry Parnell, for the Irish MPs, persuaded Parliament to allocate the money – £20,000 – for this stretch of road in Wales. Work continued from 1817 to 1820, dealing with the worst stretches first; and in 1821 the toll-houses of the Llangollen section opened for business.

The impact on Llangollen and its valley of the improved road

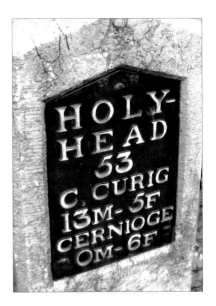

Thomas Telford   *A Telford milestone on the A5*

Telford's road, subsequently the A5, still lies between the characteristic walls which he designed and built, now diminished in height by layers of surfacing.

The Llangollen Railway

Carrog

would have been even greater than it is had not Telford also developed the route from Chester along the coast, which became the A55. A railway also reached this area, a branch line coming form Ruabon (where a main line still runs between Chester and Shrewsbury) in 1865, via Acrefair and Trevor. It became part of the Great Western Railway, and survived until the Beeching cuts in 1964, closing to passengers in 1965 and to freight in 1969. Today the part of its which runs through Glyndyfrdwy and along the slope of Glyndŵr's Mount and on to **Carrog** is restored as the route of the Llangollen Railway.

The Vale of Llangollen, below Glyndyfrdwy

Chapter 6

LLANGOLLEN

A long belt of carboniferous limestone runs through northern Wales, noticeable for its pale brightness and for its laminated structure. Laid down in warm shallow seas as the shells of a vast quantity of sea creatures some three million years ago, it rises above our landform now due to the uplifting effect of compression by the earth's shifting plates. It crops up in Anglesey, for instance near Benllech, and out-crops again offshore as Puffin Island, before extending eastwards to form the Great and the Little Orme. Thence it arcs along the coast, occasionally veering inland, as at Llysfaen, before changing direction and heading south, through Denbigh (where the castle sits on it) and Ruthin, to flank the Clwydian hills on their east side and then sweep south again to culminate above Llangollen as the Eglwyseg Crags.

This high limestone scarp forms a wild country. Bronze Age farmers appear to have been the first to inhabit it. When St. Collen came to this area, a fugitive from the supernatural threats of Glastonbury Tor, there was a man-eating giantess living up here. Collen, by nature as well as by training a soldier, took his sword up to the pass and challenged her. She called on 'Arthur the Giant' (who also lived among the crags) to help her, but Collen did not give him time to reply. He cut off her right arm, but this did not put her off. She picked it up and proceeded to beat Collen with it. So he cut off her left arm as well. The spring he washed his sword in is still called Collen's Well.

At least that is what it says in *Buchedd Collen*, a medieval tale in the form of the saint's life (*buchedd*), preserved in a manuscript of 1536 some of which (though not the episode recounted here) is translated for us by Lady Charlotte Guest, as a note in her edition of the Mabinogion. There we read of Collen's

Eglwyseg crags

The high limestone scarp

St. Collen's church

Dinas Brân – the seat of the kingdom of Powys

Eliseg Pillar

Glastonbury period, and the remarkable encounter with Gwyn ap Nudd, king of the Otherworld, which led him to regard Gastonbury as an unsuitable place to carry out his Christian mission. His prayer to be led to a secluded place was answered by a dream. H was told that by taking a certain route he would find the place he looked for, and by this means, through deep valleys and over high mountains, he came to Llangollen, and there, having got rid of the giantess which was plaguing the place he founded a church.

This for a long time stood close by where the present Parish Church is now. It was actually the third church he founded, meaning that Collen was probably in fact a well-travelled missionary. Langolen in Brittany was said to be an early step in his career, followed by Colan, three miles east of Newquay in Cornwall. Here in Wales his chosen spot lies near the river, now conveniently in a prime position near the main road, forming one flank of the town. The ruins of the old church lay alongside the present, Norman, one for some time, until the wooden tower of the latter was declared unsafe in 1749 and the stones of the old one, then demolished, were used to build a new tower. The church now, airily spacious and with an air of justified self-importance, has a magnificent 15th century carved oak ceiling.

Some three centuries after the time of Collen a prince called Cyngen ap Cadell ruled over the kingdom of Powys. We know a little about him, including the fact that he was the first Welsh prince to make the pilgrimage to Rome, after the submission of Wales to Papal authority; and that he died in 855, in Rome,after a long reign. During that time he erected a stone cross in the form of a pillar with an ornamented head, in the style established by then as Mercian, in memory of his ancestor Elised. Through what is generally recognised to be a blunder on the part of the engraver the name of the pillar's subject was changed to Eliseg. Presumably Cyngen could not at that stage send it back, with the result that we have, as one of Llangollen's many valued artefacts, 'The Eliseg Pillar'.

Elised ap Gwylog, also known as Elisedd and Elise, died in

about 755, a hundred years or so before his descendant erected his memorial. It says on the pillar that he reclaimed the kingdom of Powys from the Angles, but not much more is known about him. Cyngen achieved his aim, in that his great-grandfather is known of today through his memorial. The cross gave its name to the valley above which it stands, and the valley gave the name to the Abbey which was founded in it.

The cross was once, apparently, some twenty feet high, but it has suffered a troubled life. In the 17th century Cromwell's troops pulled it down and successfully smashed up its noble cross. It was put up again, considerably shorter, by a local landowner in 1779, but by that time its inscription had become illegible. The mound was found to contain the skeleton of a tall man, unfortunately undated.

It is the inscription which is of particular interest, and it is by a lucky chance that we are able to know of it. The antiquarian Edward Lhuyd (who was then keeper of the Ashmolean Museum in Oxford) examined it in 1696 while it was still recumbent, and copied the writing which was still then partly legible. The inscription legitimised the royal house of Powys by tracing it back to Roman times. Cyngen's great-grandfather Elised it claimed was descended from Vortigern, who was the son in law of Maximus, the self-claimed Roman Emperor. It was of course common for rulers to invent for themselves an ancestry justifying their status, and indeed many royal lines in antiquity had traced their origin to gods. What is of interest here is that the line of succession from Maximus through Vortigern accords with the tradition later popularised by Geoffrey of Monmouth, and some of the other people mentioned in the inscription occur in other old Welsh texts.

The pillar stands on top of a Bronze Age burial mound, which has grassed over and spread to engulf its stone-slabbed 'hedge'. During excavations carried out in 2012 two other burials were found within it, cremated bones preserved in small stone 'cists', which are rectangular stone boxes.

The Abbey which takes its name from the cross, Valle Crucis,

Work carried out by archeologists from Chester and Bangor universities on the mound of the Eliseg pillar, in the summer of 2012

Details of the majestic ruins of Valle Crucis Abbey (Abaty Glyn y Groes)

The gravestones of the Princes of Powys at Valle Crucis

Dinas Brân

in spite of being more correctly called Llanegwest, was founded in 1200 or 1201 by Madog ap Gruffudd, then Prince of Powys. It was a Cistercian house, an order which sought out peaceful and remote spots where the monks could be a self-sufficient community. It grew to be a centre of Welsh religious life and was the burial place of its founder and his son Gruffudd and, it was said, of the poet Iolo Goch, who became the court bard of these princes' descendant, Owain Glyndŵr. George Borrow made a special pilgrimage to the Abbey ruins to see the famous poet's grave, but found when he got there that nobody there had even heard of him.

The Abbey was burnt in the same century as it was built, and largely reconstructed, so that its ruins now date from the last part of the 13th century. The remaining fragment of its cruciform church still has a noble elegance, and extensive foundations of what was clearly a major complex remain to impress us with Llanegwest's former status. It was of course brought to its present destroyed state following the Dissolution of the Monasteries in the time of Henry VIII. Now the Abbot's house, restored, houses a display, and a pleasant picnic area is established by the fishpond, which is, incidentally, the only surviving monastic fishpond in Wales.

High on a round hill not far from the valley of the cross stand the jagged ruins of Dinas Brân, so elevated and isolated as to be continually silhouetted against the sky. The 12th century castle, seat of the prince of Powys, is in such an obviously impregnable position that it is hardly a surprise to learn that it occupies the site of an Iron Age fort. During the period of Norman incursion into Wales it fell into the ownership of John de Warrenne, Earl of Surrey, who had his main seat at Oswestry and also built a new castle at Holt (which he found more convenient than Dinas Brân, which he then neglected). In spite of its commanding position and the dramatic grandeur of its ruins, which enjoy spectacular views across the Dee valley, its period of active life was limited, and it was deliberately destroyed by the Welsh during the first war against Edward I.

It is the name, in fact, rather than the reality of the ruins, which asserts the importance of Dinas Brân. It appears to be called after the god Brân, who, in Welsh mythology, was a prototype of the keeper of the Holy Grail, and indeed there are several compelling reasons for supposing that Dinas Brân itself is the model for Grail Castle. That is referred to in Malory's collection of Arthurian material, drawn from French sources, as the Castle of Corbin. It can clearly be no coincidence that 'corbin', in old French, means the same as 'brân' in Welsh, that is, crow or raven, so that the Castle of Corbin is directly a translation of Dinas Brân.

It is worth the climb to stand among these ruins. In spite of the steep drop defending it a large-scale system of ditches and ramparts surrounds its high walls, and one can still see the remains of a gatehouse and possibly a barbican to the east and the sturdy base of a tower half-way down the wall to the south. The narrow passage-way which was the original entrance is still intact. Dinas Brân, even in the shape of its present fragmented ruins, proclaims power and grandeur. It was, it is clear, a very substantial place. The two tall windows of the Great Hall on the south side look out over the Dee valley with a distinct air of dominance.

With this depth of history surrounding it, it is hardly surprising that Llangollen itself is an old and well-established town. Essentially a convenient crossing-point of the Dee, it clearly grew up around its bridge. The Dee still surges over rocks as it enters the town and contains itself just in time to pass under this noble structure. It is said to date originally from the 14th century and so held to be the oldest stone-built bridge in Wales. In its present form largely a 15th century structure, set up by a Bishop of St Asaph, it is an impressive feature in itself. Many of the inns and houses date from the 17th and 18th century, demonstrating that Llangollen was rich and important even before the construction of the road which now runs through it. In fact it was a centre of the wool industry, like Bala, and there were times in British history when that association was enough to guarantee succes.

The climb to Dinas Brân

The bridge over the river Dee at Llangollen

Plas Newydd, Llangollen

Plas Newydd detail and the 'Ladies of Llangollen'

That Llangollen was of some importance even before Telford is evidenced by the tales of travellers of the 18th century. John Byng, whom we encountered at Corwen, stayed at the Hand, which he says had the better of the two Llangollen harpers. He visited Valle Crucis, 'a place of such curiosity and beauty that a daily visit would be a pleasure', and admired the river flowing under the great bridge, 'a deep, quick and fantastical current'.

Sure enough the Reverend Bingley too is in Llangollen in the last years of the century, but he is overtly critical of it: a 'dirty, ill built, and disagreeable town'. He disliked its narrow streets and dark shaly stone. He had to admit, however, that it was delightfully situated.

Bingley walked around the Vale and admired the Dee and the mountains. He mentions, though he appears not to have visited, the Ladies of Llangollen, (the term by which George Borrow refers to them). Plas Newydd, their 'charming retreat', Bingley says, 'has of late years been probably too much intruded upon by the curiosity of the multitudes of tourists who every summer visit Llangollen.' George Borrow mentions that they had lived in their house Plas Newydd 'for nearly half a century' and become 'celebrated throughout Europe'.

No-one can ever have set out with less success to become recluses, since the Ladies had a constant stream of visitors. It is a puzzle to us now to understand why, but we have, I think, to consider the forms taken by celebrity over the centuries of changing fashions.

Everyone who mentions them refers to the fact that they were (as Borrow says) 'of high rank'. Lady Eleanor Butler was the aunt of the young Earl of Ormond; Miss Ponsonby was the grand-daughter of General Ponsonby. Evidently these connections counted for something in the third quarter of the 18th century.

Lady Eleanor certainly came from a distinguished Irish Catholic family, though Sarah Ponsonby was perhaps not so well-off. They met at school in Kilkenny, when Sarah was thirteen and Eleanor twenty-nine. A romantic friendship developed out of their mutual dissatisfaction with their lives at home, and in 1778 they ran away together. One does not wish to pry into the private lives of people of a different period, with different tastes and standards: but there is no doubt from the portraits of them that they dressed as men, and their escape was always regarded as an elopement.

The first time they ran away they were apprehended by their families, but later that year succeeded in getting consent to leave Ireland and resort to Wales. They settled in lodgings in Llangollen, and liked the town so much that they decided to rent a cottage, Pen-y-Maes, which they set about improving and renamed Plas Newydd.

On the face of it there is nothing particularly interesting about either the lives or the characters of these two eccentrics, and it is difficult to see why their fame was so widespread or their visitors so distinguished. They lived intentionally quiet lives, away from social interference, almost never leaving Plas Newydd for more than a day. Their main occupations were writing letters, reading, and tending the improvement of their house and garden. They corresponded with Edmund Burke, Lord Byron, Lord Castereagh and George Canning. Assuming the portraits of them to be as flattering as possible they were certainly no beauties, nor did they apparently aspire to be. They dressed in identical suits of black riding clothes with top hats. In spite of these several discouragements they were visited by the great and famous, including the Duke of Gloucester, William Wordsworth, Sir Walter Scott, and even the Duke of Wellington.

The house and its setting provide some element of explanation. In the distance is a view of Dinas Brân, and wooded hillsides hide any sight of the town in between. The garden and grounds fall to a dell bearing a tributary of the Dee, the stream Cyflemen. The seclusion and the subtle way the organised landscape merges with natural country give an immediate sense of peacefulness. Wordsworth,who had a feeling for such things, wrote a poem in the grounds:

A stream to mingle with your favourite Dee,
Along the Vale of Meditiation flows...

The Ladies, highly literate and evidently discerning, are reported as saying they could write better poetry themselves. They also took exception to a patronising reference later in the doggerel to their house:

...where faithful to a low roofed Cot
On Deva's banks, ye have abode so long...

Wordsworth was not invited again. Yet the cottage was at the time quite small, though not particularly aptly termed 'low roofed', and one wonders how it accommodated the rich and royal with, presumably, their servants. It was extended by the addition of wings by later owners, and these were removed as unsound in1963 to restore the house to much the finished form in which the Ladies left it. When Lady Eleanor died in1829 they had been there together for nearly fifty years, and Sarah Ponsonby remained there alone for a further two before dying herself.

Some of the colour of the International Eisteddfod held annually at Llangollen

The main attraction of the house is its wealth of oak carvings, which were the customary gifts of their eminent visitors; and its grounds, which fall steeply to the gurgling stream. The whole has a pleasing atmosphere of intimacy. The property changed hands a number of times, after the demise of the Ladies, until bought by the District Council in 1932.

Bingley mentioned 'the multitude of tourists' who come every summer, and that was before the end of the 18th century; by the end of the nineteenth we find A.G. Bradley, in his *Highways and By-ways in North Wales*, reporting that in the August holidays 'traps and even the fearsome char-a-banc invade the leafy lanes'. Now of course this is to be expected, and it must be said that Llangollen has managed the increase in popularity well. At almost any time of the year it is busy with tourists, but particularly of course at the time of the International Eisteddfod, for which it is world-famous. This monumental feast of folk music was founded in a modest way in 1946, and is now the largest event of its kind world-wide.

Besides this achievement, its major claim to fame, Llangollen now has several survivals of its past which are put to good use for modern tourism. The Llangollen railway, a steam service, is the residue of the branch line which arrived here in 1862. The restored section owes its existence, and success, to the efforts of enthusiasts, and it is hoped that its present (2012) run to Carrog will eventually be extended to Corwen.

Just as the steam trains run partly on the fuel of nostalgia, so Llangollen's other transport link, the canal, evokes, with its horse-drawn barges, the aroma of the past. This end of the Ellesmere Canal was of course practical in its origins, taking heavy goods such as coal and iron from the Ruabon and Wrexham area, and no doubt slate from up the horseshoe pass above the town, to join the national canal grid at Hurleston Junction, where it becomes the Shropshire Union Canal.

Once again the enormously successful canal facility owes a debt to Thomas Telford. He was essentially a civil engineer, and one of his special skills was in getting means of travel and

*The Llangollen Steam Railway
Station*

The Llangollen Canal

A barge on the Llangollen canal

Pontcysyllte

Water is carried over the aqueduct in a narrow trough, scarcely wider that the boats which use it.

transport across uneven terrain. His fame and success were a product of the match between his ability and the demands of the time, sine one of the major effects of the introduction of mass-production by the Industrial Revolution was the need to transport raw material over large distances. More bulk could be moved with the same expenditure of energy, literally horse-power, on water than on roads. Hence the need for the network of canals, and once again Telford was in the right place at the right time.

Poncysyllte is a monument to all these factors, including the confident decisiveness of the time. Faced with the problem of conveying the Ellesmere canal across the Dee valley Telford took it straight across. Carried on a stone structure supported by eighteen slender pillars, it makes its leap of 1007 feet in a trough only slightly wider than the barges which still slide across it. It was built over a period of ten years, cost £47,018, and was opened in 1805 with a ceremony attended by an estimated 8,000 people.

Apart from the renewal of the railings, faithfully copied from the original, it remains as Telford built it. Your boat glides through the sky, one hundred and twenty-one feet above the Dee valley, tightly encased in a cast-iron trough, as you are carried out of Llangollen towards England.

Chapter 7

HEAVEN ON EARTH

Perched above the valley which contains the river Ceiriog, **Chirk** clearly stands at the edge of something. The road falls suddenly out of the town and cascades towards the river and the English border. It is thought that perhaps the name (which is not reflected in the Welsh name for it, *Y Waun*, meaning the meadow or moorland) is cognate with the familiar Gaelic word 'kirk', meaning church. At any rate there was a church here as early as the eleventh century, as witnessed by the Domesday Book, though the first church (perhaps much earlier than that) seems to have been a Celtic foundation, dedicated to its founder, St Tysilio, and it is evidence of the tidal flow of Norman influence across the river Ceiriog that it changed its dedication to those more familiar to the Catholic church of Europe at the time, St Mary, and latterly St Mark.

The original Norman church was what is now the south aisle, the north aisle being added, along with its tower, at a time, it is thought, of increasing church attendance, in the late 15th century. The church's interior as a whole is dominated by the ornate but at the same time elegant memorials to the might of the Myddleton family, which furnish the south aisle and flank the altar.

The Myddletons have been the strongest influence on Chirk since Sir Thomas bought the castle in 1595. He was a merchant adventurer, dealing in sugar in the Netherlands and then in Antwerp, and he brought the sugar business to London in the 1580s. He sponsored numerous commercial voyages in that decade, and crucially entered government with a lucrative post in the customs and excise which enabled him to become a financier, in the business of sponsoring trading voyages and other enterprises. His son, the second Sir Thomas, became a prominent

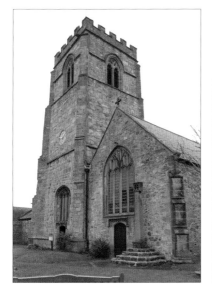

Chirk church, the canal aqueduct and the railway bridge

Chirk on the A5 was a traditional gateway into northern Wales – the Moreton Park Centre is a landmark offering local produce and heritage information

Chirk castle

Caption

Cromwellian general during the Civil War.

The castle was old by then. It was built by Roger Mortimer between 1295 and 1310. Mortimer rose to become a Marcher Lord during the reign of Edward I, being granted the lands around Chirk after the confiscation of territory of the Welsh princes. He was among the most powerful of Edward's subjects, but (in the mysterious way of the Middle Ages) fell out of favour, and only regained his status on the accession of Edward II. As a result he makes an appearance in Marlowe's play as 'the Elder Mortimer'. Following an unsuccessful rebellion against Edward he ended his days in the Tower of London.

Many great seats loom imposingly, but most seem in their old age to have come to terms with their past. Chirk Castle looks as if it is still furious about something. It crouches, squat and sturdy, on its eminence, looking out warily on the lands around: austere, severe, formidable.

This expression of its purpose, the stern reality of being a border fortress which it has had since its origins, is in odd contrast to the mellow, civilised parkland through which it is approached. The spacious spread of parkland trees and rolling meadows leads to an avenue of stupendous oaks, sublime in their venerable maturity, followed by a band of mixed woodland leading suddenly to the presence of the castle itself. All this however is first anticipated by the Davies Brothers' gates, all twirls and emblems, confronting you past the point where the road veers and narrows into the winding Dyffryn Ceiriog. Built between 1712 and 1719, by the famous firm we have noted in the chapter on Ruthin, the gates have over the centuries moved around various parts of the park, and have occupied their present position since 1888. The gates prominently feature the wolf's head which forms part of the Myddleton coat of arms, a reference to the Welsh tribal leader Rhirid Flaidd (part of whose name comes from *blaidd*, a wolf), from whom the Myddletons claimed descent.

The castle was much damaged in the Civil War, when it was taken, in 1643, by the king's troops. The Myddletons in due course got it back, and repairs took place followed by improvement, during the 17th century. In the 1670s the east side was converted into the Long Gallery, ironically a piece of Gothic revival within this authentically Gothic building. In the next century the state rooms were adapted to a classical style, and the staircase added; and in the 19th century Pugin, who had been largely responsible for the design of the House of Lords, remodelled the great hall in, again, a Gothic Revival style.

Splendid in its style and grandeur, Chirk Castle proved in the end unsustainable, and the National Land Fund (precursor of the National Heritage Memorial Fund) rescued it in 1978, and later, in 1981, transferred it to the National Trust, in the care of which it remains. By then the Myddlletons, who had let it in 1911, were back in residence, having returned during World War Two, the property having been occupied in between by Lord Howard de Walden, as tenant, a man who had made much money from London property, principally as owner of the Marylebone estate.

We are always conscious, at Chirk, of being on the border, and indeed Offa's Dyke runs through the park of the Castle. The castle itself looks out into England (Bingley says, in the last years of the 18th century, that it has a view of seventeen different counties) though it stands principally as the guardian of the entrance to the Ceirog valley, a world which could not possibly be more Welsh. A narrow and winding lane leads into it, which conveys the implicit message 'no coaches please'.

The **Ceiriog valley** came to national attention when an attempt was made to destroy it. It is the old matter of a shortage of water on the part of industrial English towns, a situation which seems to contain the assumption that because Wales had plenty of water it can be expected to give it away, regardless of the effect that this process may have on its communities and landscape. A number of north-west English towns, under the leadership of Warrington, applied for a scheme, in 1923, to turn a part of the Ceirog valley into a reservoir. This would have submerged 13,600 acres of land, obliterating the villages of Tregeiriog and Llanarmon Dyffryn Ceiriog. As the MP for Denbigh, J. C. Davies,

The great gates, by the Davies brothers, at the edge of Chirk Castle's park

Offa's Dyke near Chirk

The Glyn Valley Hotel at Glyn Ceiriog

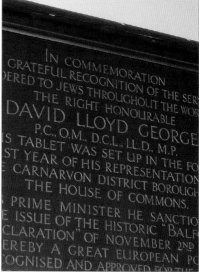

The memorial hall at Glyn Ceiriog, and the plaque to remember that the valley was saved from drowning

said in the House of Commons, the 'Warrington Corporation Bill' of 1923 would have destroyed

three villages, one church, five chapels, two burial grounds, two public elementary schools, two post offices, two inns, six shops, and 82 other dwelling houses ... denuding the valley of practically every human habitation throughout at least five miles of its length

A fund supported by the *Western Mail* backed a campaign, which Lloyd George fronted, and it was in the course of this that he pulled off the sort of magic at which he was adept: changing the world by the force of rhetoric. '*...dipyn bach o'r nefoedd ar y ddaear*', he said of Dyffryn Ceiriog: a little bit of heaven on earth.

The winding road hugs the line of the chattering river, snaking under the hills which form its banks. It is above **Glyn Ceiriog**, really. that the valley comes into its own, a fairly sudden tightening of scenic density. Rather, it contracts and expands, often tightly enclosed, sometimes broadening out into upland pasture, where it earns its supposed nickname of Little Switzerland.

In the past this terrain which is now, to us, plainly idyllic, has been put to commercial, even to industrial, use. Quarrying and mining developed out of its mineral wealth, of both slate and limestone, testament to its close-packed complex geology, and these industries gave rise to what was once its main innovation: the Glyn Valley Tramway, *Trên bach y Glyn*, originally a gravity and horse-drawn system which carried slates from above Glyn Ceiriog down to Chirk, where the transport route connected to the canal, from 1873. This converted to steam in 1887, and for a time carried passengers as well. The quarries closed in 1933, and the line itself closed in 1935, and only a few remnants, consumed into present use, can be found of it now.

Throughout this period of development, and no doubt before and after it, the valley had a home-grown cottage industry of weaving. Woollen cloth spun from the product of another local raw material, the upland sheep, gave rise to mills powered by that constant bubbling flow which is never more than a few yards away, in this tight valley. Though most of this activity took place in farmhouses and cottages, still the buildings of some fulling mills survive (along with those of other mills) beside the water-power.

Although the Ceiriog valley clearly cannot have been a mail-coach route, because it leads to a dead-end, there must be some explanation for its periodic old inns – The Swan at Pontfadog, The Glyn Valley hotel at **Glyn Ceiriog**. These and other signs (such as the substantial Madog's bridge at **Pontfadog**) remind us that the valley was more used in the past than it is now as a through route, notably on drovers' roads to Oswestry and Shrewsbury markets. Hence it was that (for instance) George Borrow came this way, on an excursion from Llangollen. A hollow way leads through the woods and descends to **Llanarmon Dyffryn Ceiriog**, and this is perhaps a remnant of the passing of the drovers. People have in fact come this way from time to time, disturbing the valley's reticence, as when, for instance, in 1165, something happened.

Henry II, king of England, had responded to the needs for assistance of the lords of Chester and Shrewsbury, whose lands wee increasingly threatened by the power of Owain, king of Gwynedd. Henry came with the royal army to Oswestry, and onwards to confront the Welsh forces at Corwen. Although massively outnumbering the Welsh, he then made a tactical mistake. He marched his forces through the Ceiriog valley.

At that time the valley was densely forested. Indeed even today an area of the upper valley, though mildly wooded now, is known as Ceiriog Forest. Henry realised the danger of this, and set two thousand woodmen to work clearing a road through it. But the combination of the surrounding trees and the constricting valley made the English army vulnerable, and by the use of traditionally Welsh guerilla tactics Owain's troops ambushed them, near to where Offa's Dyke crosses the valley at the mill below Chirk Castle, at the Battle of Crogen, where Henry nearly lost his life.

Ceiriog valley

The narrow part of the valley near Crogen

Ffordd y Saeson – 'the English track', remembers the huge army that had to retreat after being defeated by Owain's army and the Berwyn mountains

The Hand at Llanarmon

What was left of the English army struggled out of the deep valley and onto the Berwyn mountains. But there he was vulnerable to another type of Welsh weapon, the weather. It was summer, but the chronicler is explicit:

And then there came upon them a mighty tempest of wind and bad weather and rains, and lack of food; and then he moved his tents into England.

The Battle of Crogen set back the English ambition of conquering Wales, and in effect Henry (no doubt shocked by his experience) did not try again.

At **Pontfadog**, in a field above the village where it is difficult to view and on private land, stands a tree which Henry's foresters did not fell, though it must have been ancient even then, being now some one-and-a-half thousand years old: the oldest oak in Britain, dating from the reign of Egbert in the early ninth century, now measuring about forty foot in girth. Probably even more venerable are the yew trees which almost smother the church at Llanarmon, (though the present church, a replacement of 1846, is contrastingly young). These archaic monsters clearly date from a period very early in the founding of Christianity, if not before that, perhaps having been saplings in the days of the founding saint, St. Garmon, possibly Germanus himself.

These neat little nucleated villages punctuate the course of the valley, but the only place resemblling a town is Glyn Ceiriog. Here the memorial hall, housing a museum, quite rightly reminds us of another dimension of human achievement, the valley having given rise to two significant poets native to it, and to another who made it for a time his home.

Of these the most interesting historically is the earliest, since Huw Morus flourished at a critical time for Welsh culture, the second half of the 17th century. The effects on the culture caused by the Acts of amalgamation of the 1530s took a generation or so to show in the style of Welsh art: with the adoption by the Welsh gentry of English fashions and aesthetic values the long tradition of courtly literature eventually began to die out. Huw Morus, born in Llangollen in 1622 and brought up in the Ceiriog valley, worked at the time of transition. Thus he was sponsored, in the old fashion, by established landowners, such as, in this case, the Myddletons of Chirk Castle; and although he used the formal verse-forms of the tradition, such as *cynghanedd* (a form of internal assonance within the line of verse), he experimented with verse free of accented metres. His subject matter meanwhile was concerned with the everyday lives of normal people of the time.

Morus was famous in Wales in general, and George Borrow's visit to his homeland, Pont-y-Meibion, between Pandy and Tregeiriog, was something of a pilgrimage. He engages a miller's workman, to his own surprise, on old Welsh literature:

> After a little time the man asked me if I had heard of Huw Morris. I told him I was well acquainted with his writings...

He set off then to visit the birthplace, as he supposed, of the famous poet. In the process he describes for us the Ceiriog valley:

> The valley is very narrow, huge hills overhanging it on both sides, those on the east side lumpy and bare, those on the west precipitous, and partially clad with wood...

Through this terrain, and with much further difficulty, he finds the chair traditionally used by the bard, a stone construction set into a wall, and there recites some lines of Morus's poems. Huw Morus, in fact, occupies a whole chapter of Wild Wales, testament to his importance to, at least, Borrow, and for his largely pastoral poems concerning love and nature he is still much loved. Eos Ceiriog, his nickname, refers to the sweetness of his lines: the Nightingale of Ceiriog.

Dyffryn Ceiriog had to wait then for some two hundred years for another poet to arrive on the stream's banks, but then two came along at once. Robert Elis (born in 1812) actually came from

The church at Llanarmon Dyffryn Ceiriog

Huw Morus'memorial

John Ceiriog Hughes' memorial window at Canolfan Ceiriog

Pen-y-Bryn at Llanarmon, birthplace of Ceiriog

Montgomeryshire, where he was for a time a farm labourer; he joined the Baptist church in 1632 and as a Baptist minister moved to a succession of parishes. He was minister at Glyn Ceiriog in the 1840s, about which time he published the poem which made him famous, *Yr Adgyfodiad*, 'the resurrection'. His best-known work is the Ceiriog-based lyric *Cywydd y Berwyn*. A *cywydd* is a strict form of Welsh verse governed partly by the number of syllables per line.

Under his bardic name of Cynddelw (a reference to the 12th century poet Cynddelw Brydydd Mawr), Elis became a prominent literary figure at eisteddfodau and in literary periodicals, and he not only preached but lectured widely.

The memorial hall at Glyn Ceiriog, formerly a community centre, was opened as a museum in 1933 and has the principal aim of commemorating the area's poets, in particular Dyffryn Ceiriog's most admired offspring, John Ceiriog Hughes. Hughes was genuinely indigenous, born (in 1832) in a farmhouse overlooking the village of Llanarmon Dyffryn Ceiriog, at the head of the vallely, but he spent the first part of his life away, working as a clerk for railways in Manchester and London, and rose to the rank of stationmaster, which was his occupation when he returned to Wales.

Ceiriog, as he was known, his bardic name, was a prolific writer and gained much popular attention through his interest in old Welsh folk music. He set words to many traditional tunes, and was responsible for now well-known versions of, for instance *Dafydd y Garreg Wen*, and, at least in some cases by attribution, the Welsh words to The Men of Harlech, The Ash Grove, The Bells of Aberdovey, God Bless the Prince of Wales, and All Through the Night.

Ceiriog was, however, a more serious influence in the history of Welsh culture than this popularity would suggest, since he set in motion a trend towards simplicity of form and language which Welsh verse had not for some time been willing to adopt. This freed Welsh poetry to confront and deal with the realities of the surrounding world in a way which had been achieved, in

England, by the surge of the Romantic movement. His poems are strongly felt, strongly expressed, the danger of verging on the sentimental held in check by their evident sincerity.

Aros mae'r mynyddau mawr,
Rhuo trostynt mae y gwynt.
Clywir eto gyda'r wawr,
Gan bugeilliaid megis cynt.
Eto tyfa'r llygad dydd,
O gylch traed y graig a'r bryn,
Ond bugeiliaid newydd sydd
Ar yr hen fynyddoedd hyn.

Unfortunately a literal English translation falls short of conveying the honest directness of these words; nor can the lines easily be conveyed into English verse form. But it means: the mountains, and the winds around them, endure – as do the human and natural activities upon them, the shepherds singing and the daisies flowering among the rocks and hills. But these are new shepherds now amongst the old mountains.

In this slight sample from his considerable output (which comes towards the end of the long verse sequence called Alun Mabon) his aim of simplicity and unsophistication is well exemplified. The language could hardly be simpler, the verse form that of popular ballad, but the pleasant, accessible, lilting, singing manner and mood conveying this perennial message one cannot help feeling reflect, along with much else, the mood and manner of his delightful valley.

Llanarmon at the head of the Ceiriog valley

Bibliography

BINGLEY, Rev. W., *North Wales*,1814, reprinted by
Denbighshire County Council.

BORROW, George, *Wild Wales*, Oxford University Press, 1920.

BOSWELL, James, *The Life of Samuel Johnson*, Dent, Everyman, 1928.

EVANS, Lindsay, *The Castles of Wales*, Constable, 1998.

GODWIN, Fay, and TOULSON, Shirley, *The Drovers' Roads of Wales*,
Wildwood House, London, 1977.

KENYON-THOMPSON, Keith, *Welcome to Rhuthyn*, Spread Eagle
Publications, 1986

SENIOR, Michael, *This is Where You Live*, Gwasg Carreg Gwalch, 2007.
   Disputed Border, 1989.
   The Story of the Dee in Wales, 1900.